Located in Paducah, Kentucky, the American Quilter's Society (AQS) is dedicated to promoting the accomplishments of today's quilters. Through its publications and events, AQS strives to honor today's quilt-makers and their work and to inspire future creativity and innovation in quiltmaking.

EXECUTIVE BOOK EDITOR: ELAINE H. BRELSFORD
BOOK EDITOR: LINDA BAXTER LASCO
COPY EDITOR: CHRYSTAL ABHALTER
ILLUSTRATIONS: BECKY CAMPBELL
GRAPHIC DESIGN: SARAH BOZONE
COVER DESIGN: MICHAEL BUCKINGHAM
QUILT PHOTOGRAPHY: CHARLES R. LYNCH

Attention Photocopying Service: Please note the following—Publisher and author give permission to print pages 8-31.

Additional copies of this book may be ordered from the American Quilter's Society, PO Box 3290, Paducah, KY 42002-3290, or online at www.AmericanQuilter.com.

Text © 2014, Author, Becky Campbell
Artwork © 2014, American Quilter's Society

American Quilter's Society
PO Box 3290 • Paducah, KY 42002-3290
Fax 270-898-1173 • email: orders@AQSquilt.com

Library of Congress Cataloging-in-Publication Data Pending

MW01076397

Cc

Me

Quilt Construction 2

Innovative Appliqué 4

Finishing Touches 7

Patterns

Meet the Author

Becky Campbell

I have been sewing for years. I started making my own clothes, progressed to prom dresses, and then to my wedding dress. I moved on to household items, curtains, pillows—whatever I happened to need. I also decorated our house with all sorts of needlework. Always excited to learn new skills, I took a quilting class in the early 90s. I fell in love. So much to learn, so little time.

I became comfortable making traditional quilts, so I ventured into art quilts. Talk about stretching my skills! There are so many ways to do things, so many products, so much to try.

I discovered that I liked to design products and projects. I designed Sewforever Quilt Storage to provide a better way to store quilts. Then I devised Innovative Appliqué to make appliqué more enjoyable for everyone, increasing accuracy and eliminating time-consuming tasks. In order to be able to share my Innovative Appliqué techniques, I needed original patterns to work with. This led to developing patterns for appliqué.

Quilting is a skill that can always be expanded. Fabric is my paintbrush and imagination my background. The ability to combine these elements into something memorable is always the challenge.

To learn more, visit my website, Facebook page, or contact me directly.

http://www.sewforever.com
http://www.facebook.com/SewforeverQuiltingbyBeckyCampbell
Becky@sewforever.com

Quilt Construction

Constructing Plant Your Own Garden, 69" x 69"

Yardage

- 3¾ yards block background and setting triangles
- 2½ yards—sashing, outer border, and binding
- 1¼ yards—contrasting fabric for the accent
- Fabric in a variety of colors and values for the appliqué
- 4½ yards—backing
- 77" x 77"—batting
- See Innovative Appliqué (page 4) for additional supplies.

Cutting Instructions

All strips are cut across the width of the fabric.

1. Cut 4–13½" background fabric strips. Cut these strips into 12 squares 13½" x 13½". This size allows you to trim the blocks after your appliqué is complete, cleaning up the wear and tear on the edges.

2. Cut 2–22⅞" strips of background fabric. Cut 2 squares 22⅞" x 22⅞". Cut the squares once on the diagonal for the 4 corner setting triangles. Label and set aside.

22⅞"

3. Cut 1 square of background fabric 21⅞" x 21⅞". Cut the square twice on the diagonal for the 4 side setting triangles. Label and set aside.

21⅞"

4. Cut 21–2½" strips from the sashing fabric (for both the sashing and borders). Label and set aside.

5. Cut 32–1" strips from the contrasting accent fabric. Label and set aside.

6. Cut 8–2½" strips from the binding fabric. Label and set aside.

Making the Appliqué Blocks

1. For each block, make an overlay copy of Pattern A, following the instructions under General Information (page 4). This overlay will be used as a placement guide for centering the flower designs on-point in each of the background squares.

2. Complete the appliqué following the Innovative Appliqué directions (pages 4-7).

3. Trim the blocks to measure 13" x 13", remembering to keep the appliqué centered.

Contrasting Accent for the Appliqué Blocks

1. Cut 16 of the accent strips into 48 strips 1" x 13".

2. With right sides together, line up the edge of a 1" strip with one edge of the appliqué block. Sew with a **½" seam allowance**. Yes, that is ½"! Press the accent strip away from the block. Repeat this process on each side of all the blocks. You will now have a ½" narrow accent on all sides of the blocks that will later become a perfect ¼" narrow accent when you add the 2½" sashings.

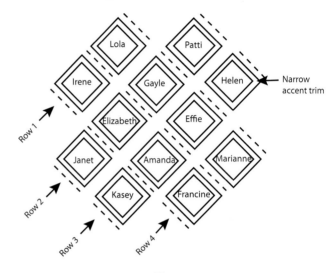

Figure 1

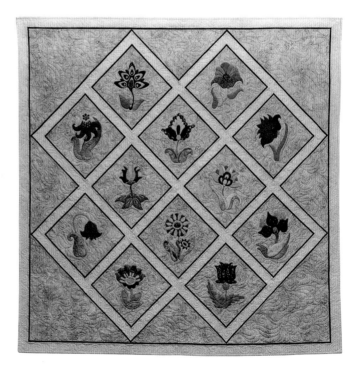

Sashing & Setting Triangles

1. Cut 6 of the sashing strips into 16 strips 2½" x 13".

2. Lay out the blocks in rows as shown (Figure 1), positioning a sashing strip between the blocks as indicated by the dashed lines.

3. Join the blocks and sashing strips in each row with a **¼" seam**. Now you will see the perfect ¼" narrow accent appear. Do not join the rows yet.

4. Check that Rows 1 & 4 each measure 31 ½". Cut 2 sashing strips 31½" long.

5. Sew one of these sashing strips to the top edge of Row 1 and the other to the bottom edge of Row 4 (figure 3).

6. Cut 2 – 1" x 31½" accent strips. Sew one to the top edge of the Row 1 sashing with a **½" seam**. Press away from the row. Repeat, sewing the other accent strip to the bottom edge of the Row 4 sashing (figure 3).

7. Cut 8 accent strips 1" x 15½".

8. Sew an accent strip to one of the short sides of a side setting triangle with a **½" seam**. Press away from the triangle. Sew a second accent strip to the remaining short side with a **½" seam**. Press as before. Repeat these steps with the remaining side setting triangles (figure 2).

9. Sew a side setting triangle to both ends of Rows 1 & 4 as shown (figure 3).

10. Sew the long edge of the corner setting triangle (the bias edge) to the upper end of Row 1 with a **¼" seam**. Sew the other corner setting triangle to the lower end of Row 4 with a **¼" seam** (figure 4).

Joining the Rows

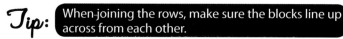

Tip: When joining the rows, make sure the blocks line up across from each other.

1. Check the length of Rows 2 & 3. They should each be 60½" long. Join 2½" sashing strips as needed to cut 3 – 60½" strips.

2. Use one of the 60½" sashing strips to connect Rows 2 & 3, sewing the strip to the lower edge of Row 2, then to the top of Row 3, with a **¼" seam**.

3. In the same manner, add sashing strips between Rows 1 & 2 and between Rows 3 & 4.

4. Cut 2 accent strips 1" x 31 ½". Sew an accent strip to each of the remaining sides with a **½" seam**. Press as before.

5. Add the 2 remaining corner setting triangles with a **¼" seam** (figure 5).

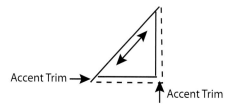

Figure 2. Dashed lines indicate the sashing strip placement.

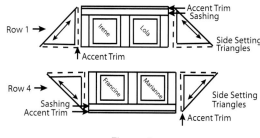

Figure 3

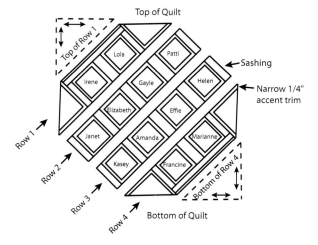

Figure 4

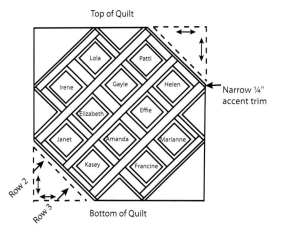

Figure 5

Outer Border & Finishing

1. Measure the length and width of your quilt top. Both measurements should be the same.

2. Join 1" accent strips as needed with 45-degree seams in order to cut two strips 1" x the length of the quilt top. Sew 1 accent strip to the left side with a **½" seam**. Press as before. Repeat for the right side.

3. Measure the width of the quilt top. Join 1" accent strips as needed with 45-degree seams to cut two strips 1" x the width of the quilt top. Sew to the top and bottom of the quilt top with a **½" seam**.

4. Measure the length of the quilt top. Join sashing fabric strips as needed to cut 2 strips 2½" x the length of the quilt. Sew a strip to each side with a **¼" seam**.

5. Measure the width of the quilt top including the sashing fabric border. Join sashing strips as needed to cut 2 strips 2½" x the width of the quilt. Sew a strip to the top and bottom with a **¼" seam**.

6. Layer the quilt top, batting, and backing using your preferred method. Quilt as desired.

7. Join the 2½" binding strips with 45 degree seams. Fold in half lengthwise, wrong sides together, and press. Add to the front edge of the quilt. Turn to the back and hand finish.

Innovative Appliqué

Innovative Products That Make the Process Easy

Additional Supplies for Turned-edge Appliqué

- C. Jenkins™ Freezer Paper Sheets, 8½" x 11", available at most quilt shops. These are heavier than freezer paper on a roll and work well in an inkjet (NOT laser) printer. This product eliminates numerous tracings.
- Roxanne™ Glue-Baste-It temporary basting glue, available at most quilt shops. The new accordion bottle design is the best choice.
- Print n' Fuse™ inkjet fusible sheets, available at most quilt shops. This product is used to create the 3-D effect.

Additional Supplies for Fusible Appliqué

- Print n' Fuse inkjet fusible sheets

Additional Supplies for Both Methods

- June Tailor® Perfect Piecing Transparent Foundation Sheets used for an overlay; available at quilt shops or Jo-Ann Fabrics and Crafts® stores
- Printable transparency film, used as a design tool; available at office supply stores (optional but useful)

General Information

If you don't own an inkjet copier/printer, gather your pattern, C. Jenkins Freezer Paper Sheets, Perfect Piecing sheets, Print n' Fuse, and printable transparency film and visit a friend with one. Steps 1–3 can be completed in 10–15 minutes.

1. Create an overlay of Pattern A for each block by copying it to June Tailor Perfect Piecing Sheets. This transparent overlay is your guide for placing your appliqué pieces on the right side of the background fabric.

2. Create a transparency preview of Pattern A (optional, yet very helpful) by copying it onto an inkjet transparency. Once the edges of the appliqué pieces are turned under, or your fusible pieces are prepared, attach them to the corresponding numbers on the transparency with a small piece of rolled tape. You can preview and change out any parts of the appliqué before sewing begins. This also enables you to audition background fabrics until you find the perfect combination (see page 6).

3. For turned-edge appliqué, copy Pattern B for each block onto freezer paper. Cut freezer-paper shapes out on the outside edge of the solid black lines EXCEPT where the dashed lines appear. Cut out about ¼" beyond the sides with the dashed lines to remind yourself to cut the fabric to extend under another piece. Place the pieces in reclosable plastic bags, each

labeled with the block name, so you don't lose anything. These freezer-paper pieces will be ironed to the front (right side) of fabrics that you choose to create the appliqué design.

Turned-edge Appliqué

1. Pick your fabrics for the appliqué pieces. You can use the photo of each quilt block as a guide or choose your own colors. For different flower parts that are the same color, use a variety of fabrics of that color to add interest.

2. Iron Pattern B freezer-paper pieces to the **right side** of your chosen fabrics.

3. Cut around the freezer-paper shapes approximately ³⁄₁₆" beyond the solid black lines and more generously at the dashed lines, as these areas will lie under another shape. Sharp fabric scissors are very important; they give you a clean edge to work with. Place all cut pieces in your labeled plastic bag.

4. To turn the edges, place the cut shape freezer-paper-side down on a cutting mat. You'll be looking at the wrong side of the fabric. I like the traction the Olfa® mat provides. The green mat protects your surface and helps you see the edge of the freezer paper.

5. Apply a THIN line of Roxanne glue approximately ⅛" in from the cut edge of the fabric facing you (the wrong side). The glue should be a little inside where the edge will be folded so you are not stitching through glue later.

6. Use a Clover® seam ripper or your favorite turning tool to turn the cut edge down into the glue. The freezer paper will hold your fabric and only the edge will turn down. I find the handle on a Clover seam ripper gives me the best control. Hold the seam ripper like a pencil. Do **not** turn under the edges with dashed lines.

7. Hold the turned edge down with your finger for a second and work around the shape. On curves, ease in the fullness to achieve a nice smooth edge.

8. At corners, fold in the tip of fabric, then fold in each side, using a dot of glue on each fold. (The side folds will form a miter at the point.) It may help to hold the tip with a pointed tool and turn the sides down with another pointed tool. Be patient with yourself. With a little practice, you will be a pro.

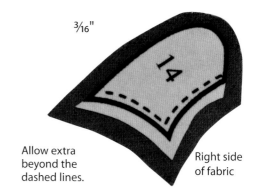

³⁄₁₆"

Allow extra beyond the dashed lines.

Right side of fabric

Step 3

Steps 4 & 5

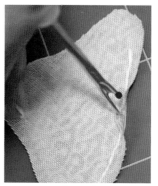

Step 6

Step 8

Applying Appliqué to Background Fabric

Transparency Preview (optional)

If you copied Pattern A to a transparency, now is the time to use it. Put a small piece of rolled tape onto the wrong side of each turned or fused piece and attach it to its corresponding numbered spot on the transparency. Carefully remove the freezer paper. Now you can preview your fabric selections to see how they work together. If you have not already selected a background fabric the transparency also enables you to preview background fabric. Leave all the pieces attached to the transparency; you will remove them in the next step.

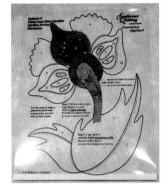
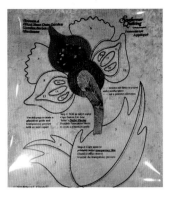

Attach the appliqué pieces to the transparency with tape. (optional)

Audition different background fabrics. (optional)

Placement

1. Use the Perfect Piecing copy of Pattern A as your placement guide. Position it on the background fabric where you want the appliqué located. Pin the copy on the left side to the background fabric so it opens like a book. It is helpful to place pieces following the numbered sequence given.

2. Apply a thin bead of Roxanne glue on the wrong side of each piece, just inside the edge of the folded seam allowance.

3. Slip the appliqué piece under the placement guide and hold it for a second. Continue transferring all the pieces to the background fabric.

If you used the transparency step, the appliqué pieces will not have the freezer paper still attached. Remove the appliqué pieces from the transparency in the numbered order and transfer them to the background fabric following the directions above.

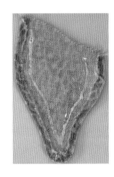

Steps 1 & 3: Attach and use the placement guide to position the appliqué on the background.

Step 2: Apply glue.

Ready to Stitch

After all the pieces are in place, begin stitching. The objective is to stitch so the stitches don't show. Match your thread color to your appliqué pieces. (The red thread in the photos is only to illustrate the stitches more clearly.)

1. Come up through the background fabric into the folded edge of your appliqué piece with your needle.

2. Pull the thread through. Your thread knot will be on the wrong side of the background fabric.

3. Needle down into the background fabric a bit underneath the appliqué piece.

4. Come up again into the folded edge of the appliqué piece about ⅛" from the previous stitch.

5. Repeat the process until the piece is completed.

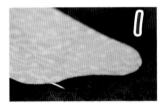

Note that even with contrasting thread, the stitches don't show.

Fusible Appliqué Instructions

Fusible appliqué results in the flower being oriented in reverse of how it appears in Pattern A. If you want your appliqué oriented like the pattern, select the mirror image, reverse mode, or flip/horizontal on your printer's settings. Place Print n' Fuse in your printer tray so Pattern B will print on the paper side.

Roughly cut out the Print n' Fuse flower shapes beyond the line, iron the shapes to the wrong side of your chosen fabrics. Press for five to eight seconds with a hot, dry iron. Let cool. Cut out the shapes on the solid black lines **except** at the dash lines. At the dash lines cut approximately ½" from the solid line to allow that area to extend under another piece.

3-D Effect Without Trapunto

1. COPY Pattern B for each block to Print n' Fuse.

2. Cut a piece of batting 8½" x 11".

3. IRON the Print n' Fuse Pattern B to the batting.

The following steps are best performed on one shape at a time.

4. CUT out the batting shapes INSIDE THE LINES so they are a little smaller and fit inside the appliqué stitching lines on the wrong side of the background fabric.

5. REMOVE the paper backing by scoring it with a pin, then peeling it off.

6. IRON the Print n' Fuse side of the batted shapes to the back of the appliquéd shapes, using the appliqué stitching as your placement guide.

Score the paper backing with a pin and gently peel the paper away for the fabric. Use the Pattern A, Perfect Piecing placement guide to position the pieces, fusible side down, on the right side of the background fabric in numbered order. I recommend placing one piece at a time. Cover with a damp pressing cloth. Set iron to wool and press firmly for 10–15 seconds. Remove the pressing cloth and iron until dry. Continue until all pieces are in place.

Sew down the edges of the fusible shapes to the background fabric with a zigzag, blanket, straight, or satin stitch.

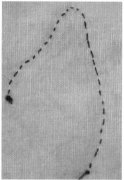

Stitches visible on the wrong side of the background

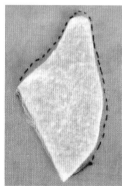

Batting-side up, with Print n' Fuse side ironed to the wrong side of the background

Finishing Touches

For a single block, add a border of your choice. Layer with batting and backing as you normally would. Quilt as desired. Add the binding, a hanging sleeve, and your label. Pick another flower to add to your garden.

For the full-size quilt, make all 12 blocks and follow the quilt construction instructions (pages 4).

Gayle
(page 16)

Elizabeth
(page 14)

Once the overall quilting is complete, go back with your sewing machine and stitch in the ditch between the individual flower parts, matching thread color to the fabric color you are stitching on. This adds dimension and keeps the batting behind each piece from shifting in the future.

Good job!

Patterns

Irene: Pattern A

Copy this page to make a place ment guide and transparency preview (page 6).

------ denotes cutting a generous allowance to extend under another piece.

Enlarge 111%

Irene: Pattern B

Copy this page for turned-edge appliqué
(pages 5-6), 3-D effect (page 7), and fusible
appliqué (page 7).

------ denotes cutting a generous
allowance to extend under another
piece.

Enlarge 111%

Please note: Tiny parts
can be painted on.

Lola: Pattern A

Copy this page to make a placement guide and transparency
preview (page 6).

Enlarge 111%

----- denotes cutting a generous
allowance to extend under another
piece.

Lola: Pattern B

Copy this page for turned-edge appliqué (pages 5-6), 3-D effect (page 7), and fusible appliqué (page 7).

------ denotes cutting a generous allowance to extend under another piece.

Enlarge 111%

Janet: Pattern A

Copy this page to make a placement guide and transparency
preview (page 6).

------ denotes cutting a generous
allowance to extend under another
piece.

Enlarge 111%

Janet: Pattern B

Copy this page for turned-edge appliqué
(pages 5-6), 3-D effect (page 7), and fusible
appliqué (page 7).

------ denotes cutting a generous allowance to extend under another piece.

Enlarge 111%

Elizabeth: Pattern A

Copy this page to make a placement guide and transparency
preview (page 6).

------ denotes cutting a generous
allowance to extend under another
piece.

Enlarge 111%

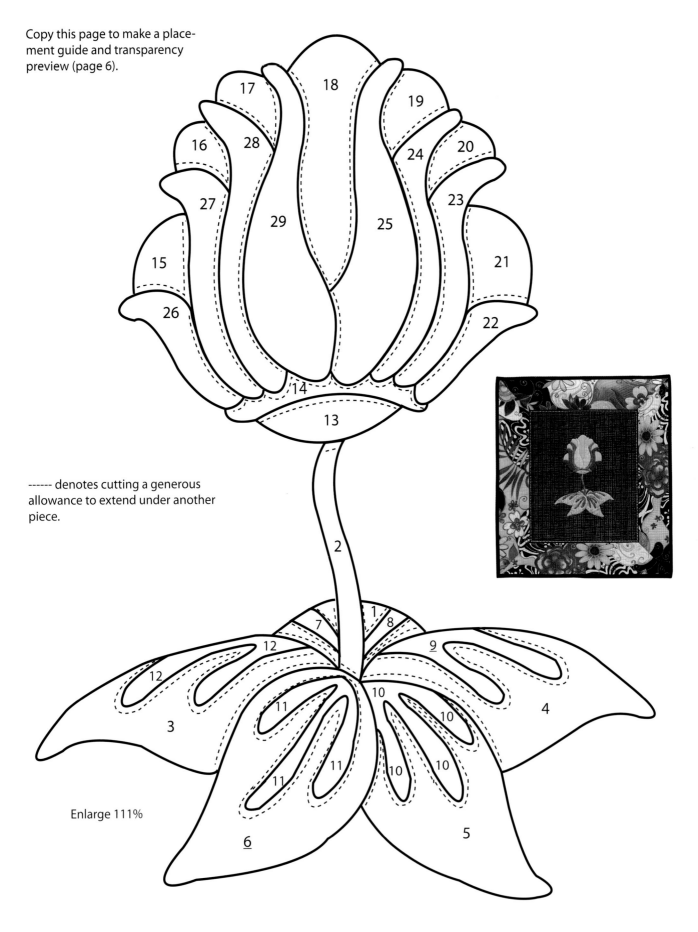

Elizabeth: Pattern B

Copy this page for turned-edge appliqué
(pages 5-6), 3-D effect (page 7), and fusible
appliqué (page 7).

------ denotes cutting a generous allowance to
extend under another piece.

Enlarge 111%

Gayle: Pattern A

Copy this page to make a placement guide and transparency
preview (page 6).

Enlarge 111%

------ denotes cutting a generous
allowance to extend under another
piece.

Gayle: Pattern B

Copy this page for turned-edge appliqué
(pages 5-6), 3-D effect (page 7), and fusible
appliqué (page 7).

------ denotes cutting a generous allowance
to extend under another piece.

Enlarge 111%

Copy this page to make a placement guide and transparency preview (page 6).

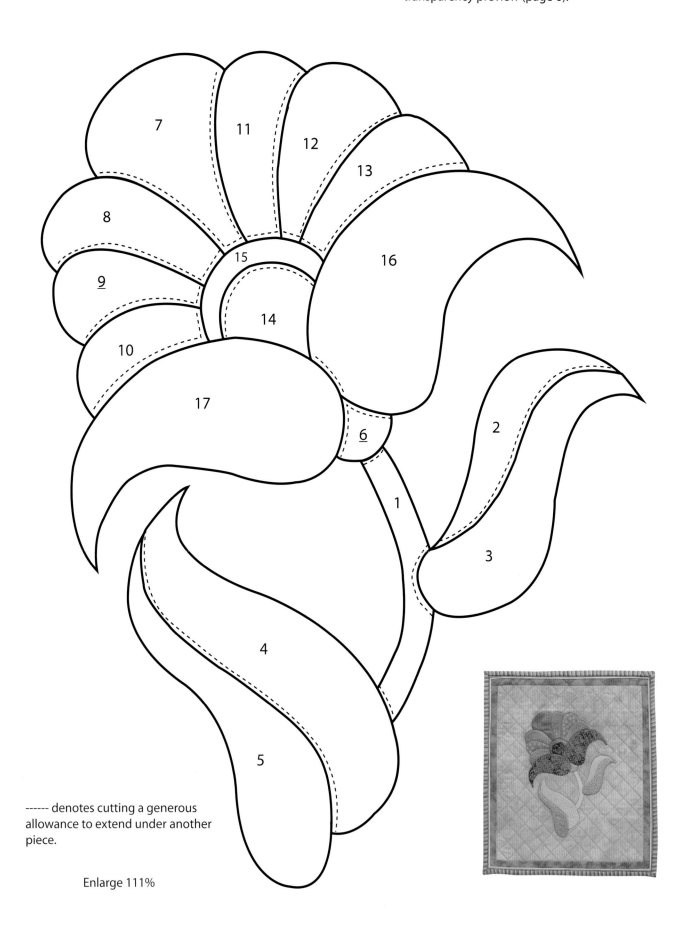

------ denotes cutting a generous allowance to extend under another piece.

Enlarge 111%

Patti: Pattern B

Copy this page for turned-edge appliqué
(pages 5-6), 3-D effect (page 7), and fusible
appliqué (page 7).

------ denotes cutting a generous allowance
to extend under another piece.

Enlarge 111%

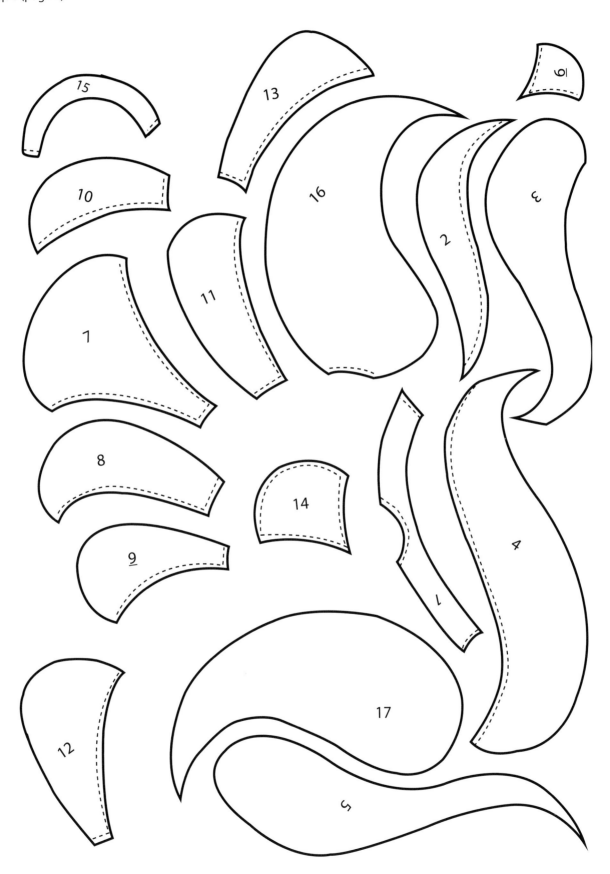

Kasey: Pattern A

Copy this page to make a placement guide and transparency preview (page 6).

----- denotes cutting a generous allowance to extend under another piece.

Enlarge 111%

Kasey: Pattern B

Copy this page for turned-edge appliqué (pages 5-6) 3-D effect (page 7), and fusible appliqué (page 7).

------ denotes cutting a generous allowance to extend under another piece.

Enlarge 111%

Amanda: Pattern A

Copy this page to make a placement guide and transparency
preview (page 6).

------ denotes cutting a generous
allowance to extend under another
piece.

Enlarge 111%

Amanda: Pattern B

Copy this page for turned-edge appliqué (pages 5-6), 3-D effect (page 7), and fusible appliqué (page 7).

------ denotes cutting a generous allowance to extend under another piece.

Enlarge 111%

Effie: Pattern A

Copy this page to make a placement guide and transparency
preview (page 6).

Enlarge 111%

------ denotes cutting a generous
allowance to extend under another
piece.

Effie: Pattern B

Copy this page for turned-edge appliqué
(pages 5-6), 3-D effect (page 7), and fusible
appliqué (page 7).

------ denotes cutting a generous
allowance to extend under another
piece.

Enlarge 111%

Helen: Pattern A

Copy this page to make a placement guide and transparency preview (page 6).

------ denotes cutting a generous allowance to extend under another piece.

Enlarge 111%

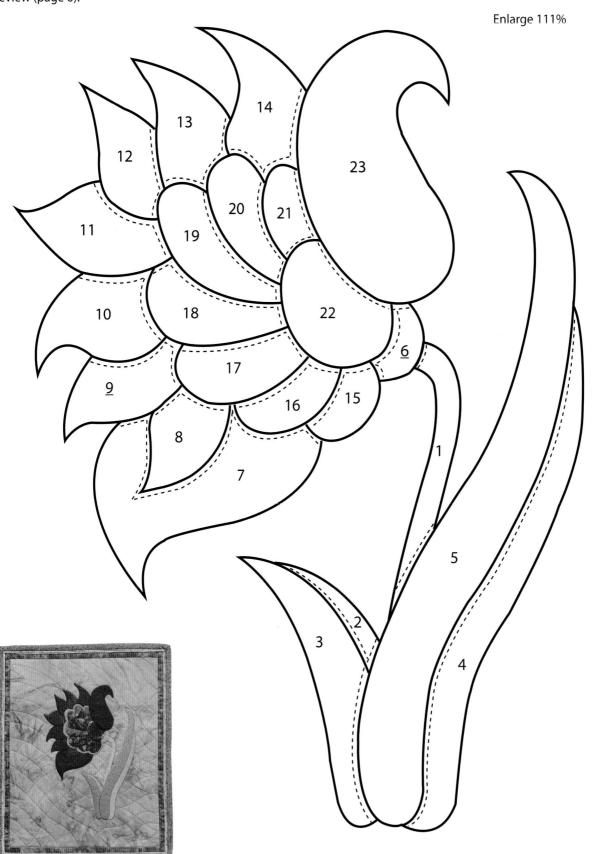

Helen: Pattern B

Copy this page for turned-edge appliqué (pages 5-6), 3-D effect (page 7), and fusible appliqué (page 7).

------ denotes cutting a generous allowance to extend under another piece.

Enlarge 111%

7

2

22

10

21

12

14

11

8

17

20

19

9

16

15

3

6

5

4

1

23

13

18

Please note: Tiny parts can be painted on.

Francine: Pattern A

Copy this page to make a placement guide and transparency
preview (page 6).

------ denotes cutting a generous
allowance to extend under another
piece.

Enlarge 111%

11

12

13

15

17

21

19

16

18

14

20

7

10

9

8

6

1

2

3

4

5

Francine: Pattern B

Copy this page for turned-edge appliqué
(pages 5-6), 3-D effect (page 7), and fusible
appliqué (page 7).

----- denotes cutting a generous
allowance to extend under another
piece.

Enlarge 111%

Marianne: Pattern A

Copy this page to make a placement guide and transparency
preview (page 6).

------ denotes cutting a generous
allowance to extend under another
piece.

Enlarge 111%

Marianne: Pattern B

Enlarge 111%

Copy this page for turned-edge appliqué
(pages 5-6), 3-D effect (page 7), and fusible
appliqué (page 7).

------ denotes cutting a
generous allowance to
extend under another
piece.

More AQS Books

This is only a small selection of the books available from the American Quilter's Society. AQS books are known worldwide for timely topics, clear writing, beautiful color photos, and accurate illustrations and patterns. The following books are available from your local bookseller, quilt shop, or public library.

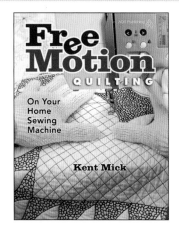

#1585 .... $12.95

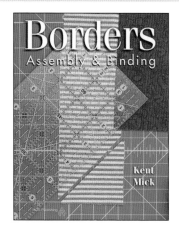

#1586 .... $12.95

#1590 .... $12.95

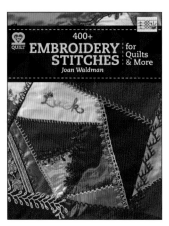

#1274 .... $12.95

#1278 .... $12.95

#1275 .... $12.95

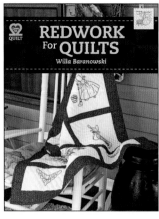

#1273 .... $12.95

#1589 .... $12.95

#1280 .... $12.95

LOOK for these books nationally.
CALL or **VISIT** our website at

1-800-626-5420
www.AmericanQuilter.com